BEGINNING

BONSAI

THE GENTLE ART OF MINIATURE TREE GROWING

by
SHIRLEY & LARRY STUDENT

CHARLES E. TUTTLE COMPANY
Rutland, Vermont & Tokyo, Japan

In the pursuit of bonsai,

search for the ideal,

where the mind, heart, and hand are one.

Acknowledgments

Our life in horticulture in general and bonsai in particular has been enriched by the many wonderful people we have met working with plants and trees. We have studied with many of the leading bonsai artists in the United States, including John Yoshiyo Naka, whom we are honored to call friend and mentor.

We express our gratitude to the bonsai teachers who have given so freely of their knowledge, sharing with us their love of this wonderful art form.

To our students and readers we express our appreciation for their curiosity, which stimulates and excites our own study.

We cannot personally acknowledge all the people who helped with the book but we wish to thank our illustrator and photographer, Robert Johnson, well-known watercolor artist and teacher.

Finally, we appreciate the support and encouragement of our daughter Toby, a bonsai artist herself, and her husband Michael, our son Michael and his wife Barbara, and our grandson Sandy, whose smile lights up the day.

Published by the Charles E. Tuttle Company, Inc.
of Rutland, Vermont & Tokyo, Japan
with editorial offices
at 2-6 Suido 1-chome, Bunkyo-ku, Tokyo 112

© 1993 by Charles E. Tuttle Publishing Co., Inc.

Library of Congress Catalog Card No. 92-80694
International Standard Book No. 0-8048-1729-4

First edition, 1993

Printed in Japan

Contents

FIG. 1 *The juniper, with its needlelike foliage and aromatic wood, makes an attractive bonsai.*

A Short Introduction to Bonsai

Bonsai is the Oriental art of creating miniature versions of nature's wondrous trees; it is the reproduction, on a small scale, not only of the dwarf trees of the mountains but also of the giant trees of the forests.

In ancient China naturally dwarf trees were collected from mountainous areas and revered throughout the country. The trees were potted in beautiful, highly decorated containers and enjoyed as "artistic pot plants," as they were then called. It is thought that little else was done to the trees to keep them alive other than attending to their basic horticultural needs. These "artistic pot plants" were kept behind palace walls for the ruling classes.

Over the centuries much of China's culture was sent to Japan. The Japanese absorbed and refined this culture, which included elements of religion, government, architecture, and the "artistic pot plants" that were sent to Japan as gifts for the aristocracy. These plants might have remained behind palace walls had not Chinese monks introduced them to the public as they taught Zen Buddhism to the common people. The miniature trees were ideal teachers of philosophical principles concerning the harmony of nature, man's place in the universe, and the harmonious blending of heaven, earth, and man. From this beginning, bonsai emerged as the horticultural art form we practice and study today.

Unlike the wealthy man, the common man could not travel to the mountains to collect trees. He had to rely on whatever was easily obtained, the trees and seedlings near his home or at the outskirts of his town or village. To these young trees he collected, he began to apply what he had seen nature do to trees over the years. He observed the wonders of nature that created strong, old trees, sometimes showing beauty, often dignity and character, and always the ability to survive.

The working class, who first saw the wonder of dwarf trees, soon began to establish the elementary guidelines of what would become a sophisticated horticultural art form. From that time on, the art of bonsai would be continually studied and expanded by its masters and their followers.

Bonsai, as we know it today, evolved from its Chinese origins into an art form that produced smaller, more refined trees. Chinese gardens were loose, free, expansive. Their "artistic pot plants" reflected that horticultural approach. On the other hand, Japanese gardening was more precise, contained, and refined. Moreover, because the space for living and the time for gardening for ordinary Japanese were limited, their tree designs and containers became smaller and more refined. In Japan, the *tokonoma*, a small ceremonial alcove, became an important part of every home. Trees were brought into the house and placed in the *tokonoma* for short periods of time.

In the past, as now, the primary concern was to keep the trees alive and healthy after they were root pruned and planted in shallow pots. The development of tree design and style would evolve slowly, but from early on, the trees that were used were small and young, and the artistic goal was to create the illusion of an old tree with strength and character.

Oriental philosophy and religion taught that the world was ordered yet asymmetrical. The concepts of heaven, earth, and man, fitting within a triangle, brought peace and harmony to daily life. These concepts formed the basis for many art forms, including bonsai. Nature's work was not to be copied exactly but to be reproduced in miniature. Unlike nature, man does not create big trees; but as in nature, man's work on his "created" tree is never complete. Each tree, whether tiny or large, is a unique creation, ever changing.

Stories are told of trees being passed down from generation to generation, a tradition recognizing man's imperfections and humble reverence for nature. A single man would not presume to think he had perfected or completed the development of a tree in a single lifetime. The study of bonsai in this book derives from the teachings of generations of masters who have spent their lives acquiring horticultural knowledge as it merged with the art of designing miniature trees.

Today the artistry and technique of bonsai are universal. With the spread of bonsai throughout the world, many species of trees from many countries have become proper subjects for bonsai. Bonsai belongs to everyone.

As you approach the study of bonsai, know that you and your trees will change. You will bring your own feelings and artistry to bonsai. The goal of your first venture into bonsai should be to learn the techniques of the art—hands on, step by step, tree by tree. Strive always for the harmony of heart, mind, and hand.

After World War II, our returning servicemen spoke with wonder and awe of beautiful Japanese trees hundreds of years old, growing in shallow pots. As it was with them, may you too be caught up in the beauty of your own miniature trees and never get over the mystery and romance of bonsai.

FIG. 2
Miniature bonsai are 10″ or under. You can grow a number of them even when space is limited.

Bonsai from Different Sources

Not enough can be said about the collecting of the naturally dwarf trees that originated bonsai. Collected trees represent many of the finest bonsai in existence in the world today. For the most part these trees are obtained from mountainous areas. Collectors search far and wide for specimens that display the protection and care of nature, as well as the fury of the elements. Well-known examples include the magnificent juniper of California, the splendid pine of Colorado, and the larch of Nova Scotia.

As stated in the previous chapter, not everyone is able to plan trips or excursions to the out-of-doors to collect trees. Moreover, trees should not be gathered by those who have not perfected the techniques needed to keep them alive. The horticultural component of bonsai is the most important area of study for the obvious reason that horticultural knowledge maintains the life of trees.

Besides collecting plants in the wild, you can obtain bonsai from seeds, cuttings, the air-layering technique, and nurseries. There are certain advantages and disadvantages to these methods.

SEEDS

Many early books recommended planting seeds to obtain bonsai samples. Following that advice, I filled dozens of small pots with seeds. My husband, taking the sight of black plastic pots everywhere as a sign of my serious interest in bonsai, bought me a complete set of bonsai tools. With pruner in hand, I sat and waited for something tall enough to make a cut on. What a waste of time for the novice! The time would have been much better spent working my hands in the soil, or working on trees that had enough development to allow me to practice pinching, pruning, and wiring. Although obtaining bonsai from seeds may sound appealing, it takes a very long time to obtain specimens large enough to work on. However, planting seeds is a good way to obtain unusual trees.

CUTTINGS

Making cuttings of plant material is a convenient method of propagation. Almost everything can be easily rooted, except pines and some of the other conifers, which require a specific schedule for taking cuttings to be rooted.

With a clear plastic box (available in housewares departments) and two inches of moist sand in the bottom, a jar of rooting hormone containing a fungicide, and a sharp knife or scissors, you are ready to begin rooting. The box keeps cuttings moist and does not require you to think about daily watering and misting. Place the box in strong light, but not in the sun, as the sun will cook the contents. You will know when your

cuttings are rooted, since the clear box will allow you to watch the root development.

A cutting should have four to six healthy leaves. No leaves should be on the stem inserted into the damp sand. Cuttings taken when new growth hardens, before it turns woody, root more easily. As you become more adept, you will want to take thicker cuttings and cuttings with interesting shapes.

AIR LAYERING

This technique allows you to select a branch that looks like a tree and root it while it is still attached and being nourished by the parent tree.

In the spring, select the desired branch. With a knife, cut one-third of the way into the branch, just below a leaf node. Nature will want to start healing this wound as soon as the cut edges meet, so keep them separated by inserting a toothpick. Dust the cut area with rooting hormone containing a fungicide, then wrap it with damp, sphagnum moss. Next, wrap the moss with plastic, and close the top and bottom with twist-ties. When the plastic has filled with roots, cut the branch off just below the root system. Remove the plastic and moss and then pot the rooted branch.

The same process can be used with a branch that reaches the ground. Make the cut on the bottom of the branch, insert a toothpick to keep the cut open, gently place the cut area in a hole in the ground, and cover it with soil. Roots should develop. If necessary, place a rock on the branch to keep it in place. Cut the branch from the parent and pot it when it has rooted.

NURSERY STOCK

The quickest and in many ways the best way to get started in bonsai is with nursery stock. As already implied in this chapter, most beginning students are very interested in working on their bonsai—pinching, pruning, and wiring—and beginning with nursery stock provides that opportunity.

Most bonsai people eventually become involved in various methods of propagation. You will probably find that there is always something you would like to have, that often seeds are available, or a friend is willing to give you a cutting. Browsing in garden centers and greenhouses becomes part of the lifestyle of many bonsai aficionados. By browsing and buying when you see desired material, you end up always having pots of plant material waiting to be worked on. This stockpile provides a fine opportunity to broaden your knowledge by observing plant material in various stages.

BUYING BONSAI

Today there are many bonsai nurseries and retailers offering quality trees and supplies. Sales personnel at a good bonsai nursery will inform you about the environmental and care needs of your trees, especially the matters of light, water, and winter storage. They will give you the proper name of the tree you choose to ensure that you can seek additional information from others, as well as do your own research.

We get many phone calls requesting information about trees the owners do not know the names of, though they usually assure us that their trees have green foliage! Needless to say, such information is almost useless, and in such cases we can give only general information instead of a specific response. By all means, get the proper name and any other available information about a plant when you buy it.

Unfortunately some trees come with wrong or misleading information. One common example is a phrase like "keep it moist," which means almost nothing and too often misleads people into overwatering. When you are given vague information like this, you must ask questions until you completely understand how to take care of the plant you are talking about.

The day you buy a tree, you have to pay some attention to the weather. In winter, be sure the tree is wrapped for protection against the cold. A tree cannot be left in an unheated car while you continue your shopping. In very warm weather, trees left in cars can cook.

When purchasing a tree, look for good color and freshness in needles or leaves. Also, the size of the tree should be right for the pot. Many trees are planted in pots that are too large, resulting in watering problems.

Before you leave the retailer, you should know what kind of light the tree requires. Outdoor placement in the right light should be no problem because of the many choices of location you have.

An indoor tree should be placed by a window that receives the proper light for that species. Bonsai are living, growing trees and cannot be placed permanently on bookshelves or coffee tables. They are objects of artistic design, but their horticultural needs come first.

BONSAI BY MAIL

Beware of ordering a bonsai or kit from a catalog house that is not a nursery. Photographs of plants are often misleading, and too often trees are not the size or age indicated on advertisements. Chances of survival are slim. Avoiding this type of purchase saves you not just money but the disappointment of losing a bonsai. This warning does not apply to established nurseries that publish catalogs, advertise in bonsai periodicals, and stand behind the trees they sell.

Bonsai Publications and Organizations

The following well-known publications can assist students of all levels:

> *Bonsai: Journal of the American Bonsai Society*
> ABS Executive Secretary
> Box 358
> Keene, NH 03431
>
> *International Bonsai*
> William N. Valavanis
> PO Box 23894
> Rochester, NY 14692-3894
>
> *Bonsai Clubs International*
> Virginia Ellermann
> 2636 W. Mission Road #277
> Tallahassee, FL 32304
>
> *Bonsai Today*
> W. John Palmer, Publisher
> Stone Lantern Publishing Co.
> PO Box 816
> Sudbury, MA 01776

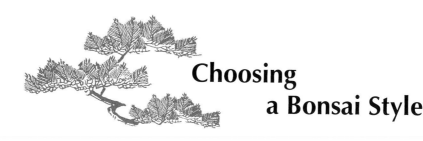

Choosing a Bonsai Style

As bonsai evolved, designs that use the trunk, branches, and surface roots in the most natural way became the art's classic styles. In the transition from China to Japan, designs became more clearly defined, emphasizing balance as well as beauty. This refinement of bonsai styles was the result of pinching, pruning, and wiring. In the dwarf trees he worked on, man reflected what he saw in the trees around him. The art of bonsai continues to be refined even today.

As many trees lend themselves to more than one style of bonsai, you have to decide how you want to design your tree. It is important to approach a tree to be worked on with an open mind, to look carefully at the trunk and branches. Every plant has its own character. The ideal is to bring out the best tree from a certain piece of material. As our Japanese bonsai masters remind us, "Bend like the willow, not like the oak."

In creating bonsai you concentrate on the trunk and on the placement of branches. By doing this, you create an essential part of bonsai design—negative space, the space between the branches, the open area that allows "little birds to fly through." In the finished design there should be a harmony between the parts of the tree and the open space.

There are many more bonsai styles than those shown but the following should serve as models to inspire you to create trees with good balance and pleasing design. Viewing different styles should stimulate your creativeness and make you aware of the individual parts (the trunk, branches, etc.) that make up the whole tree. But though established styles provide invaluable models, they do not tell the entire story of bonsai. At no time should you hesitate to design a bonsai just because it does not conform to an established style. Remember that a good bonsai is one that draws the viewer into the tree and reveals the wonder of nature.

STYLES OF TREES

Trees growing in nature are formed by the elements. Wind, storms, and the need for light cause trunks to move from the straight, upright style. The following sketches remind us that trees adjust to the environment that nature has placed them in, be that environment gentle or harsh.

1. straight upright (FIG. 4)

The tip of the tree is directly over the base of the trunk. The tree has a well-defined branch structure.

2. curved upright (FIG. 5)

The tip of the tree is over the base of the trunk. In between, the trunk has developed a long, gentle curve.

3. slanting upright (Fig. 6)

The tip of the tree has grown away from the base of the trunk and is over the soil mass. The tree must be stable and not appear about to tip over.

4. windswept (Fig. 7)

The leaning trunk, branches, and foliage show the effect of constant wind.

5. semicascade (Fig. 8)

The tree has more slant than the slanting-upright trunk. Often the trunk extends across the pot, and slightly beyond the edge of the pot. The foliage may occur below the rim of the pot.

6. cascade (Fig. 9)

Think of this as a tree clinging to the side of a cliff. The trunk line is flowing downward. The cascade bonsai should be put in a container specifically designed for that style of bonsai. The container represents the cliff from which the tree grows.

7. grove (Fig. 10)

An uneven number of trees is planted together. See Chapter 6.

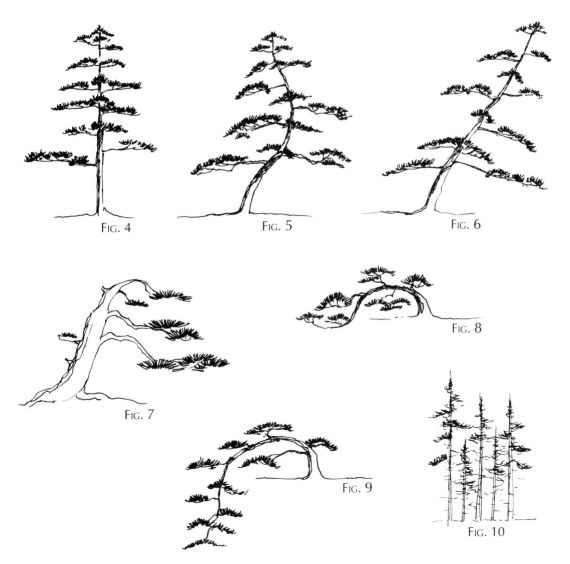

Fig. 4

Fig. 5

Fig. 6

Fig. 7

Fig. 8

Fig. 9

Fig. 10

4

Essential Techniques and Materials

Today more and more people are living in apartments in large cities, surrounded by more blacktop than green space. For such people the rewards of bonsai are especially great. Central to successful bonsai are the actions of pruning, pinching, and wiring.

PRUNING

Pruning enables you to shorten the height of a tree, remove unwanted branches, and shorten others. Bonsai are pruned with the same basic techniques used for pruning other trees.

An example of unwanted material within a tree is crossed branches, which should be removed. A tree flows from the inside out, with new growth developing outward in an uncluttered line. All branchlets growing inward, toward the trunk of the tree, should be removed. However, before cutting off an unwanted branch, be certain it cannot be wired to an area where it is needed. In the sketches of bonsai in this book, unwanted branches have been removed.

Also absent from the sketches are signs of youth, including "sucker growth," branchlets growing straight up or straight down from the main limbs. On the main lower branches, the foliage from the trunk a third to half way out the branch is missing. This is where age, lack of light, or lack of nutrients causes foliage loss. Since this loss occurs natu-

rally over the years, removing this lower foliage adds the illusion of age to young trees. Loss of inner foliage occurs less on the tree's upper portions, where branches are younger. No loss occurs on the new growth at the top of the tree. This area, of course, is young and vigorous, and receives full light.

The best time of the year for pruning is late winter or early spring. As spring can come early or late, you should pay close attention to the change of seasons in your own locale.

How to Make Cuts

The most important tool for making cuts is pruners, which should be sharp and clean. If pruning is a new experience for you, get plenty of practice before beginning to work on your bonsai. For practice, prune outdoor shrubs or branches collected from the woods. If the pruners were a Christmas gift, you can get a lot of useful experience by practicing on a discarded Christmas tree. When you are pruning, keep in mind an image of the tree you desire.

To remove a branch, place a pair of concave pruners close against the trunk, and make a sharp, flush cut. Do not tear the branch.

To shorten a branch, make a cut just above the fork of the branch. Whenever it's possible, make the cut toward the back so the cut will not show. When shortening a branch, you can very often choose the direction of new growth that will occur on the branch. If you want the new growth to follow a line on the left of the branch, prune above the bud on that side. Pruning above the bud will allow the bud to "break," resulting in new growth where you want it. Prune as close as possible to avoid leaving an unsightly stub, but do not press so close that you injure the bud. Practice finding the bud and pruning near it without injuring it. As you get used to pruning, you are bound to gain confidence.

Pruning begins the process of changing a tree in a pretty container into a bonsai. Pruning also makes your tree healthier, allowing light to fall on all its parts. If a dark area is apparent, especially an area that is difficult to see, correct the problem at once, as the area will become weak over time due to lack of light. Wire and reposition branches from dark areas into light areas.

Severe pruning is usually not done in the fall. To survive the winter, trees store energy and food in their various parts. Do not change that balance by unnecessary pruning. Indoor tropical bonsai, which go through a moderate dormant period, may be pinched and pruned when they send out new growth.

PINCHING

Pruning and pinching go hand in hand for the health and beauty of the tree. Pruning is done with scissors and pruners; pinching is done with the fingers.

Pinching is a natural process, as no plant can support all the foliage it produces. A plant either sheds completely, as deciduous trees do, or sheds the older, inner foliage it produced several years before, as conifers do. By pinching new growth, you nourish older growth, ensure new bud formation, and avoid ending up with branches that are bare except for green tips.

Fig. 11

This sketch shows a branch as it would appear if you were looking down on it. Notice that the thickest, longest branchlets taper down in size, giving the branch the triangular shape that occurs naturally in many trees. In this sketch, half of the branch has been pruned. That half is now ready for pinching. With your fingers, you would remove all growing tips on the pruned half of the branch, those outside the triangle's left line.

Fig. 12

This sketch shows half of a tree pruned to expose the best view of the trunk, as well as lower branches that have shed their inner foliage due to age or lack of light or nutrients.

Pinch new growth as soon as it appears. Do not let it grow and become woody. Deciduous and leafy material should be pinched after two to four new leaves have opened. Always leave some leaves and nodes on each branch. Coniferous new growth pushes out in clusters of needles. Pinch as the clusters start to open. Grasp a cluster with one hand, and pinch about half of it with your fingertips, using a grasp, twist, and pull action. If a branch needs to be longer, do not pinch it until the desired length has developed. *Juniperus procumbens nana* should be pinched in the spring, when it explodes into new growth. Pines are better left for later, after you have more experience. Pines are not as forgiving as many other species, especially since they do not bud up on old wood.

Pinching should be ongoing, as new growth will continue to appear as long as the plant lives. Pinching all these growing tips nourishes dormant buds, causing them to start growing. Later, pinch those, and the cycle continues. The development of twigs, twiglets, and lots of side growth results in a fine bonsai.

By pinching and pruning you control the growth cycle and hence the growth of your bonsai. Once you decide on the height and width of your tree, keep growth and development within your design. Do not allow the tree to grow out of that design.

WIRING

In some ways you use wire the way an artist uses a paintbrush. Wire permits you to design the tree you envision, enabling you to create natural, flowing lines as you reposition branches. Branches growing above each other can be wired to allow sunlight to reach both. A gentle curve can be put in the trunk, or the trunk can be straightened.

Study your tree carefully to determine which parts require wire to achieve the shape you desire. Do not hesitate to use wire. Even at those times when you are unsure whether or not to wire a branch, wire it. The wire can always be removed if it is not needed.

Different sizes of wire are used on different parts of trees. In general, use 1.5 or 2 mm aluminum-coated wire for branches and branchlets, and 1 mm wire for very thin branchlets. For heavier branches and trunks, use 2.5, 3, 3.5, 4, or 5 mm wire.

As for length, cut a piece of wire one and a half times the length of the branch to be wired. When applying the wire, do not try to shape the tree, but concentrate on putting the wire on. Wrap the wire with one hand, and support the trunk or branch being wired with the other hand. Both hands should move together up the tree. Later, when you shape the tree, again use both hands, one hand doing

FIG. 13
You will need different sizes of wire for different types of trees and different parts of the same tree.

the shaping and the other hand supporting the part of the tree being adjusted.

The wire goes onto the trunk first, then onto the branches, and finally onto the twigs, if needed. Start at the bottom of the tree and work up and out. Always anchor or secure the wire, so that when you begin shaping it the wire will hold what you are wiring where you want it. When wiring the trunk, insert the wire into the soil directly behind the trunk. When wiring a branch, take two or three turns around the trunk before you begin to wire the branch.

The wire should be put directly on the surface being wired, but not so tight to bruise it. Loose wire, wire that allows free space between the wire and the bark, will not provide the strength to shape the tree, nor will it hold the part of the tree you have worked on in position.

Neatly applied wire, the technique of which comes with practice, does not detract from the tree's appearance. Apply the wire at a 45° angle, an application that works well and also looks good. However, you will have to adjust the angle to accommodate branches and twigs.

The wire should be checked often to make sure it has not cut into the bark. If it looks like it has, remove the wire by cutting it off with your wire cutters. It is always better to rewire a branch than to scar the bark of the tree.

If the wiring is successful and the bonsai holds the desired position when the wires are removed, no further wiring is required. On young material, the position of the wired trunk or branches may be set after a full growing season. But if there is movement after the wires have been removed, or the desired shape is not attained, rewire the plant.

When you are shaping it, the tree should be a little on the dry side, so it will be less turgid. This means that it will have less water in the trunk, and the

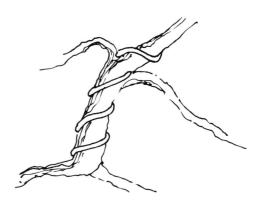

Fig. 14
When wiring the trunk, insert the wire in the soil behind the trunk.

Fig. 15
When wiring a single branch, stabilize the wire on the trunk.

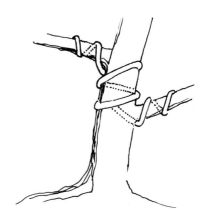

Fig. 16
You can use one wire to shape two branches.

branches will be more flexible. Of course, not all plants can be wired the same way. Some species are naturally brittle and should be shaped with care. Gently test branches for movement and brittleness by moving them with your fingers.

When removing wires, do not attempt to unwire. It is safer to take blunt-nose wire cutters and cut the wire along the curves of the trunk and branches. Just let the cut pieces of wire fall off.

Refining the tree to the desired shape can be done over the next several days or weeks. Move the branches gently, a little bit at a time. Occasionally it is necessary to put on a second wire to accomplish the results you want. The second wire should follow the same line as the first wire.

To practice wiring, cut a branch from a tree growing in your yard. The branch should resemble a tree with a trunk and branches when held up. Insert the branch into a block of wood in which a hole has been drilled to hold it in an upright position. Practice brings confidence, and soon you will be wiring with ease.

The Wire to Use

The two most common types of wire used for bonsai are aluminum-coated wire and copper wire, neither of which harms the tree. Today aluminum-coated wire is more popular than copper wire, which was the wire of tradition. Aluminum-coated wire is easier to use because it is more flexible. However, aluminum-coated wire does not have the holding power of copper wire, so you must use a heavier weight than you would if you were using copper. Copper wire may still be preferable when you are wiring heavy, older trees.

Wire, like other bonsai supplies, is more readily available now than previously. In a hardware store, check the electrical-supply section for copper wire.

BONSAI CONTAINERS

Dwarf trees evolved from the "artistic pot plants" of China, eventually becoming the bonsai of Japan. Their containers also underwent considerable change, the most obvious being the change from the ornate, decorated pots of China to the more subdued pots of Japan. Pots also became smaller, to accommodate smaller plants. Today pots made in

---

Fig. 17

Pot collecting is not only fun but also ensures that you will have different sizes and shapes to select from for your bonsai.

Japan set the standard as the finest bonsai containers in the world.

Bonsai students are naturally attracted to pot collecting, since a variety of sizes and shapes ensures having the proper pot when it is needed. Choose a pot with a size and shape that harmonize with the tree you are raising.

A terra-cotta pot, unglazed and brown in color, complements many trees. This type of pot most resembles the earth, and the color does not detract from the tree. The unglazed pot also has the advantage of not cracking in temperatures below freezing when trees are in winter storage. Glazed pots, if frozen, may crack, or the glaze may separate from the clay.

Trees that require winter storage must be removed from glazed pots. Remove the tree with the root system intact, and wrap the root ball in aluminum foil. Make a few drainage holes in the bottom of the foil so the water will drain out. The tree can then be stored.

Colored glazed pots should be used selectively to enhance the color of the foliage of flowers. One popular color for glazed pots is cobalt blue.

Most styles of trees look natural when planted in rectangular or oval containers. Bonsai containers are usually shallow, as shallowness enhances the tree's

trunk. Slender trunks look stronger in shallow pots. Heavy trunks require deeper pots. A two-inch-diameter trunk often needs a pot two inches deep to bring out the best of the trunk. How-

FIG. 18
This pot is too small for the tree.

FIG. 19
This pot is too large for the tree.

FIG. 20
There is a good balance between the pot and the tree, and the position of the tree in the pot.

F<small>IG</small>. 21

The pot was selected to enhance the beautiful curved trunk as it sweeps across the soil mass. The tree is Juniperus chinensis shimpaku kishu.

ever, a trunk with a diameter of one-half inch will not look right in a pot one-half inch deep, especially if the plant is tall and slender. View oversize containers with caution. In most cases they hold too much soil for the root systems of trees.

When looking at bonsai containers, be sure to choose one with adequate drainage holes. Never plant anything in a container without drainage holes.

Selecting the right pot for a tree requires experience, study, and a variety of pots to choose from. With regard to price, remember that harmony between tree and container is your goal, and that the plant will live in the chosen container for many years.

INTRODUCTION TO TOOLS

Bonsai tools, like the tools for any craft, should help you accomplish your work in the quickest and easiest manner. In particular, cutting tools, which come in many styles and sizes, are instruments that allow you to make cuts that do not harm or disfigure the tree.

Choose tools that are well balanced and comfortable in your hand. Buy the best you can afford. With proper care, well-made tools last a lifetime. Keep them clean, free of rust, and sharp. Quality tools stay sharp longer and are more easily sharpened than inexpensive tools.

Shears and Scissors

Cutting tools are a must for bonsai growers. Bonsai scissors are designed to cut at all points, from the tips of the blade to the V. The tips let you get into a tree without having to open the blades wider than is necessary. This allows you to remove unwanted foliage with ease and at the same time avoids damaging foliage left on the tree. Many bonsai people like the larger butterfly-handle shears for cutting heavier branches.

Concave Branch Cutter

This tool, available in several sizes, is used to remove branches close to the trunk and limbs. When a branch is cut with a concave cutter, the shape of the cut allows it to heal fast. One useful tool to start with is an eight-inch cutter, as it has a good-sized cutting surface.

Tweezers

Consider a pair of bonsai tweezers as an extension of your hand and fingers. Tweezers can easily remove a leaf, needle, or small twig without disturbing other foliage on the tree. Tweezers are also great for removing growing tips. The spatula end is useful for smoothing soil, scraping moss before applying it to the soil, and tamping moss onto the soil and firming it against the rim of the container. The tweezer end, held lightly, is used to rake down the loose soil of small plants.

Chopsticks

Chopsticks that are slightly sharpened are used for tapping soil into, around, and under a root ball that has had excess soil removed, has been root pruned, and has been placed in a pot. Tapping the root ball's soil helps stabilize the tree in the pot, remove air pockets, and smooth off the soil around the base of the tree.

Root Rake

The root rake is used for loosening and removing soil from the root ball of the stock plant when you are preparing to put the tree into a bonsai pot. By raking down the top, sides, and bottom of the firm root ball, you remove spent soil and expose the roots to be cut.

Wire Cutters

Bonsai wire cutters have a rounded head to prevent damaging the bark, therefore allowing you to get close to the branch or trunk to cut wire. Cutters come in various sizes. The thicker the wire to be cut, the larger the cutter needed.

Jin Pliers

This tool is used to create special effects like *jin* and *shari*, discussed in Chapter 10. Grip this tool as you would any pair of pliers and run it along the dead portion of the branch. The pliers will loosen the bark and allow you to peel it off easily.

Other Tools

As your trees become heavier and thicker and you work on larger material, your skills will become more advanced and you will want to add to your tool collection. Heavier pruners and shears will allow you to make cleaner cuts and will not tear at the plant. A clean cut not only looks better, but makes for a healthier tree. As you begin to use heavier wire, heavier wire cutters will also be needed.

Also available are various sizes of branch benders, or levers, which are used when a large trunk or branch, in addition to being wired, must have additional pressure to bend it slowly into a different position. Actually the bender works as a combination vise-lever, moving the branch or trunk until it attains the desired placement.

Another tool to consider is a folding

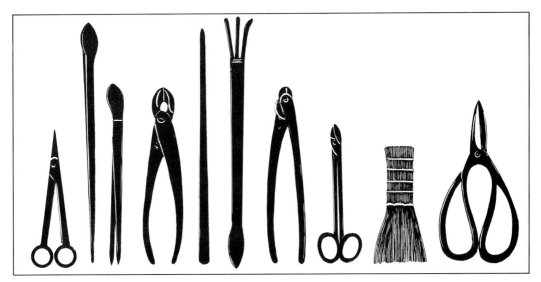

Fig. 22 *Tools shown are bud scissors (shears), long tweezers, tweezers, concave pruners, bamboo chopstick, root rake, large wire cutters, wire cutters, brush, and butterfly-handle shears.*

saw, which is useful for removing a large branch close to the trunk. The folding saw is also good for working on a heavy root system. Saws of several sizes are a must when you collect trees.

Taking good care of your tools is an important part of successful bonsai growing. Do not use your bonsai tools for anything other than working on trees. Keep an old pair of scissors on hand for cutting screen and other chores.

SOIL MIXES

When ten bonsai people get together to discuss soil mixes, you end up with ten different "recipes" for the ideal mix. Thus, the subject of potting mix can become complicated and confusing, but there is no need to let that happen.

Potting soil should support your tree in two ways. First, the soil should have enough texture to stabilize the tree in the container. (Refer to the explanation of chopsticking in the At Home section of Chapter 5.) Second, the soil should be a mixture that stimulates the feeding roots that supply nutrients to the tree.

A basic soil mix should be easily understandable and readily available, and should allow you to grow all types of bonsai, with minor adjustments for different species of trees. The mix should drain fast, so most water passes through and does not sit in the container. However, some water retention should occur. Texture is an important element, for the roots need something to hold onto to provide stability for the tree. Nutrients are another important element in the basic mix. The soil you use should also be clean and insect-free.

In most outdoor areas the soil down where the roots are growing looks dark and rich, has texture from decaying matter, and lots of small stones and grit from erosion. View this as a basic soil mix.

Roots develop in a quick draining soil,

one that allows the ongoing exchange of moisture and air. When root tips sense dryness (air), they begin to move, seeking moisture. As they rub against sharp objects like small stones, they divide and go around them. Roots surrounded by water do not have to move to find a water source, but instead of increasing, they begin to rot away. All water and a lack of air amounts to suffocation.

The basic mix of equal parts of loam, humus peat moss, and coarse sand meets the needs of most trees. The loam provides nutrition. The humus peat moss retains moisture and supplies various stages of decaying matter as texture for roots to hold onto. The most important ingredient is the sand, which must be coarse, with lots of little stones and grit. Do not use fine sand, as it will make the soil unusable. Poultry grit or aquarium gravel can be used in place of sharp sand. Do not use beach sand or anything else suspected of containing salt.

The basic soil mix can be adjusted for climate and type of plant. In very warm, dry climates, peat moss provides more moisture retention. In cold, damp climates, additional sand allows the soil to dry more quickly. For bonsai like pines that require more dryness between waterings, increasing the sand allows for quicker drainage. Bonsai maples, which suffer leaf burn during hot spells when planted in shallow containers, benefit from extra peat moss in the mix.

There are many soil mixes and various individual ingredients, but the ingredients described here—loam, humus peat moss, and coarse sand—are familiar, inexpensive, and readily available.

In most areas soil mixes are offered already bagged and sterilized, and are available under many trade names. Usually they do not list their ingredients. Many contain mostly water-retaining components that permit slow drainage.

Soil varies from place to place, and a

book like this one cannot begin to describe the differences. Search out information about local soil conditions, and rely on advice from your garden center.

FERTILIZER

It is a myth that bonsai are kept small by being starved. When bonsai are actively growing, they require fertilizing, not so much to stimulate new growth but to maintain health. Nutrients are used up and washed out of the soil during watering. Like soil preparation, fertilizing is a subject that can become very complicated, but, again, that is not necessary.

The three major ingredients in fertilizer—nitrogen, phosphorous, and potassium—provide for the most important needs of trees. These ingredients are indicated by three numbers that appear on a package of fertilizer. The first number indicates the amount of nitrogen, the middle number the amount of phosphorous, and the last number the amount of potassium. If a fertilizer is called all-purpose, it also contain small amounts of the trace elements.

Nitrogen promotes healthy green growth. Phosphorous is important for the development of inner structure, and also promotes heavy flowering and fruit production. Potassium seems to develop disease-resistant plants. The trace elements, which vary somewhat according to the brand of fertilizer, provide nutrients for plant health and growth.

A mixture of 20-20-20, i.e., all three numbers the same, is considered nitrogen feeding, and is good for all green growth. A mixture of 15-30-15, or phosphorous feeding, is used on trees like *Serissa foetida* that flower all year. If flowers occur once a year, as with azalea, both formulas should be used, one to nourish green growth, and the other when the plant is setting flower buds.

There are many fertilizers to choose from, and many people believe that an occasional change of diet is a good idea. The most convenient fertilizers to use are water-soluble and are applied as the soil is watered. Never fertilize the plant when the soil is dry.

Fertilizers prepared for regular-size plants are too strong for bonsai; cut the amount given to bonsai by half. Feed every two weeks when the trees are growing actively. At the end of August you should begin slowing down the fertilizing in climates cold enough to require special winter storage for plants.

Do not feed sick trees. Feeding is for trees in active, healthy growth. Trees grown indoors may be fertilized when new growth is visible.

Outdoor trees should be fed every two weeks, as the fertilizer is leached out of the pot by daily watering. Indoor trees do not require as much feeding. Since they are usually watered with a watering can or with a sink sprayer, the fertilizer is not leached out as rapidly. Trees grown indoors can be fertilized when new growth is visible.

SUPERTHRIVE

Superthrive is a vitamin and hormone treatment that minimizes shock after root pruning, after repotting, and when seeds are planted or roots cut. After root pruning and repotting a plant, place the plant in a tray of tepid water containing ten drops of Superthrive per gallon of water. The solution should come about halfway up the pot. When the soil has soaked up the moisture, that is, when the top of the soil from the edge of the pot to the trunk is moist, remove the plant from the tray and allow it to drain.

Superthrive is not a fertilizer and should not replace a tree's feeding program. However, bonsai that appear less than vigorous should benefit from a watering containing Superthrive.

Getting Started

A garden center can be the best resource facility in your area. The staff at a good garden center should be knowledgeable and helpful, willing to answer your questions even if they have to search out the information. These answers should be given in a manner you can easily understand and should encourage you to ask more questions. Look for a center that is clean and insect-free, one with various kinds of plants that appear to be healthy and well cared for.

It is often written that out behind the garden center you will find material that has been rejected because it does not conform to the uniform look of the rest of that size and species of stock. Because a tree is different, twisted, or stunted, some people think it will make a good bonsai, but this is not necessarily true. When living material is rejected and put out back, it is no longer cared for. It should not be purchased unless you plan to cultivate it until it regains the health and vigor necessary to withstand root pruning.

A garden center offers you the opportunity to observe and compare plants. Stock plants grown in containers have numerous feeding roots and little, if any, taproot. These feeding roots are important to the tree's health. Having the roots intact in a nursery pot allows you to study the plant's root system, knowledge that is essential in bonsai.

At the gardening center you can also observe flowering foliage and fruit trees, often in several stages of their normal growth. Azaleas are a good example of material that varies greatly, both in foliage as well as in flowers. Some azaleas grow upright; others are of the spreading variety, wider than they are tall. Such variations occur in many species of woody plants. It is of great advantage to see what a species looks like in a one-gallon container, and after several years of growth, in a three- or five-gallon container. Seeing a tree at different stages gives you an indication of how a species matures.

WHAT TO CHOOSE

You should look for a tree or woody

FIG. 23

This is a one-gallon Juniperus procumbens nana *growing in a nursery pot.*

shrub with compact growth and small leaves or needles, characteristics that help improve the proportions of your overall design. *Juniperus procumbens nana* fits this description and is readily available. It is an excellent plant to start with because it grows rapidly, making it a forgiving material for the novice. Its ability to send out new growth on hardwood is another useful characteristic. Because *Juniperus procumbens nana* grows fast, it provides the opportunity to practice and learn the techniques of pinching and pruning.

Chapter 3 lists the parts of a tree to be considered when you select stock plants. You should begin with the trunk, which should be thick. Gently move the foliage away so you can select a plant with a thick trunk. At the same time, make sure you choose a plant with a multitude of branches, as that will allow you more choices in designing the tree.

Since the amount of roots pruned and the amount of foliage removed should be roughly equal, you should select the largest plant available to guarantee more than enough foliage to compensate for root pruning. Some branches will need to be pruned and others wired or pinched. Underneath all that mass of foliage, you will discover a tree that had not been visible in the nursery container. It is upon making this discovery that many people become hooked on bonsai. Another important lesson to be learned from beginning with mature plants is that you will realize all the time that is lost in waiting for cuttings or small plants to grow large enough to work on.

To try different styles of bonsai buy two or three stock plants of the same species. Having to care for plants with the same horticultural needs is easier for bonsai beginners. Also, you will become more comfortable with the techniques of design by repeatedly using them on plants of the same species. Choosing several styles of the same species gives you the opportunity to improve your ability to "find" a tree in a stock plant.

If you live in a climate where winter temperatures are freezing and below, the trees that grow naturally in your area are "outdoor bonsai." Their life cycle is based on a period of winter dormancy at temperatures natural to your areas. Many trees are lost because their owners do not understand the importance of outdoor wintering-over for those species that require it. "Indoor bonsai," tropical trees that will not survive a freezing winter, are kept indoors for the winter months.

Understanding your trees' needs is very important. Do not proceed without essential information about material you are interested in working on. In cold climates, where tropicals will not survive the winter, the garden center will keep them in a greenhouse. However, do not assume anything about the care of your trees. Ask!

AT HOME

Juniperus procumbens nana lends itself to all styles of bonsai. Do not accept only the manner in which the tree has been grown at the nursery. Wiring allows you to wire a trunk into one of the upright styles, or to create a trunk in the cascade, semicascade, or windswept style. (See Chapter 3.)

Take the tree out of the pot by gently tapping the bottom of the pot and sliding the tree out with the root ball intact. To avoid root damage, do not pull the tree out. Turn the empty pot over and place the root ball on the upturned pot. This allows you to look into the heart of the material. Make sure that enough of the trunk at the base of the soil is exposed. This can be done by removing the soil around the trunk with tweezers or gently with your fingers.

Turn the tree to view it on all sides, so

FIG. 24

Styling of a one-gallon Juniperus procumbens nana *can begin when the tree is in a nursery container.*

you can determine which is the best view of first the front, then the sides, and finally the back. Continue turning your tree, looking for the best view of the trunk. That view is where the trunk looks the strongest and gives you a feel for the overall design of the tree. The best view of the trunk will become the tree's front. Place a marker in the root ball to remind you where the front is.

Now that you have determined the tree's front, clear out all debris within the tree. Remove dead and broken branches, crossing branches, and branches growing inward toward the trunk. Remember that all growth should flow out from the trunk. Cut out young, thin branches growing below what you have chosen as your lowest, heaviest branch. Remove the same kind of growth if it obscures the view of the trunk. Also remove anything growing straight down or straight up from the main branches. Eliminating these signs of youth will expose the older wood.

Continuing this pruning will reveal

the clear, clean lines of your chosen design. With the size and design of your tree decided, now give your attention to potting the tree before the roots dry out. Keep the roots moist by wrapping them in newspaper or by misting them, but pot the tree as soon as possible.

The next step is to rake down the soil from around the trunk and all sides of the root system, with a rake, chopstick, or tweezers. Do this with a gentle raking action, not by pulling and tearing at the root system. More soil should be loosened from the bottom of the root ball than from the sides, as the root system must be shallow enough to fit into a bonsai container. When one-third to one-half of the old soil is removed and many roots are exposed, it is time to root prune. When pruning roots, use sharp scissors and make clean cuts. Do not tear the roots.

Remove heavy roots, especially those with few fibrous feeding roots. Also remove any corkscrew or wiry roots that will not allow the root ball to sit flat in the bonsai container. The inner root ball, directly under the trunk, should be compact, with many loose, fine roots all around. When placed in the container, the roots should gently spread out on all sides to receive the new soil. When potting your tree, always use fresh soil mix and be sure to discard the used soil.

As a general guide, *Juniperus procumbens nana* looks best in brown terracotta containers that are oval or rectangular. The one-gallon nursery stock usually comes in a round growing-container approximately 7¼" tall and 6" wide. The bonsai pot you will put the raked-down tree in will be about 7" long, 5" wide, and 2" deep.

Prepare the container by covering the holes of the pot with a piece of fiberglass screen about an inch larger than the holes. Next, put in a layer of small stones (about ¼" in diameter) to cover the

Juniperus procumbens nana, Japanese garden juniper

Eugenia uniflora, Surinam cherry

26

Malus, crab apple

Rhododendron, satsuki azalea

Elaeagnus commutatus, silverberry

Buxus microphylla compacta, Kingsville boxwood

Ulmus parvifolia neri, cork bark elm

Chamaecyparis pisifera squamata glauca, blue moss cypress

bottom of the pot about ⅜" deep. On top of this, place a layer of your prepared soil mix about the same depth.

Most bonsai are designed to be asymmetrical. The tree will appear more natural if placed slightly back of the center and slightly to one side. Choose the side that allows the heavier foliage to be over the wider expanse of soil. If the longest branch of the tree is on the right side of the tree, place the tree slightly to the left side in the container. This position allows the tree to look balanced in the pot; otherwise, the tree will appear to be falling out of the pot.

After the tree is properly placed in the container, cover the root ball with an abundance of fresh, loose soil. Take your slightly sharpened bamboo chopstick and, starting at the outer rim of the container, work the new soil gently under the root ball. Use the chopstick to fill in the soil around the root ball and to tamp new soil into the pot. While chopsticking, be sure to hold the trunk of the tree in the proper position so the tree doesn't walk across the pot.

Chopsticking should be done with a light, quick touch. Each time you pull the chopstick out, the hole will fill with soil. Continue to work the soil gently under and around the root ball. After a few minutes you will feel resistance to the chopstick from the added soil. Continue until the root ball is covered and the tree sits securely in the container.

Proper chopsticking of the soil is important for a number of reasons. First, it provides new soil for the fine feeding roots to grab onto as they grow. Second, chopsticking eliminates air pockets that allow for water accumulation and eventual root rot. Third, chopsticking firms up and stabilizes the tree in the pot. When a tree trunk moves in the pot, the roots are torn and new roots are not allowed to develop. Proper potting of the tree ensures its health and growth.

Place the potted tree in a deep tray or saucer, and pour in enough Superthrive solution to fill half of the pot. (As described in Chapter 4, the mixture should consist of ten drops of Superthrive per gallon of water.) Make sure the water used in the solution is tepid. The tepid water will be absorbed by the soil through the drainage holes in the pot. You will know it has been absorbed when the top of the soil is moist and dark. Remove the pot from the tray and let the excess water drain.

Place the potted tree on the upturned nursery pot and lay collected moss on the moist soil. Use thin moss, piecing it together and firming it onto the soil with the spatula end of your tweezers. Roll the moss in along the edge of the pot so the moss complements the tree. In addition to making the tree look good, the moss prevents the soil from washing away when the tree is watered.

Now is the time to continue refining your design. At this point you must be sure that enough top growth has been removed to compensate for the amount of roots pruned. At the same time it is important to leave enough foliage for the newly trimmed tree to photosynthesize and manufacture food.

Photosynthesis is the process by which a plant manufactures sugar and starches to nourish itself. The leaves of the plant, through their pores, take in carbon dioxide during daylight hours and give off oxygen at night. Sunlight falling on the green leaves of plants is absorbed by chlorophyll in the leaves, and water and carbon are converted into the sugar that feeds the plant. Photosynthesis is continuous as long as sunlight falls on the plant. Roots supply water and essential minerals. Transpiration is the process by which leaves give off excess moisture; it too occurs during daylight hours. The

A

Fig. 25-A

The selection of this tree, a one-gallon Juniperus procumbens nana, *was discussed earlier in the chapter. This example was the largest found and appeared to have an interesting trunk, as much as could be seen through the foliage.*

B

Fig. 25-B

Remove the tree from the pot and elevate it for study and observation. The more you turn the tree, looking at it from all sides, the more familiar it will become. Decide on the front of the tree, the view that shows the tree at its best.

C

Fig. 25-C

Having determined the front of the tree, begin initial pruning. This pruning will reveal the trunk and give you a better look at what is inside the foliage.

Fig. 25-D

Continue pruning to expose the clean line of the trunk. This will allow you to see not just the trunk and its movement but also the heavy branching you will have to work with.

Fig. 25-E

Further pruning shows proportion and the general line of the design. This stage should begin to set the overall size and shape of the tree.

D

E

FIG. 25-F

Begin to rake down the soil from the top and sides of the root system. The raking action should be light and quick. Do not dig and tear at the roots. Prepare the raked-down plant for the bonsai container as quickly as possible to prevent the roots from drying out.

F

FIG. 25-G

Remove more soil from the bottom to make the root system shallow. Use a bonsai container to judge how much soil to rake from the bottom of the root ball. Rake until the root ball is shallow enough to fit into the container.

FIG. 25-H

Remove the heaviest roots, as they contain few feeding roots.

G

FIG. 25-I

Prune additional roots, to leave a compact root ball. Loose roots radiating around the root ball will be covered with fresh soil mix.

FIG. 25-J

Prepare the container with fiberglass screen and stones. The screen should be about an inch larger than the hole in the bottom of the container.

H

J

I

K

L

M

N

FIG. 25-K

Cover the bottom with small stones.

FIG. 25-L

Place ⅜" of soil over the stones. When putting in soil, make a smooth, flat surface for the root ball to sit on. The corners of the pot should be filled level with the rest of the surface so they do not form indentations when watered.

FIG. 25-M

Place the tree in the container, and cover the root ball with new soil. Use a chopstick to feed soil under and around the root ball. Keep adding new soil to chopstick in. Take time to make sure soil particles are chopsticked into place and no air pockets are present.

FIG. 25-N

When the tree is firm in the container, place it in a tray filled with the Superthrive solution to half the depth of the container. Watch as the soil absorbs the liquid, first at the edge of the container and finally in the area around the trunk.

FIG. 25-O

Drain and moss the tree.

O

FIG. 26
*Remember what you
started with?*

processes of photosynthesis and transpiration enable trees (and humans) to live.

NEWLY POTTED BONSAI

The completed tree should be placed in bright light, not direct sun. Shelter it from the wind, which is very drying. Light misting of the foliage is beneficial and cuts down on stress.

Feeding roots develop when they move in search of moisture. Be certain that air has returned to the soil surrounding the root ball by checking daily how quickly moisture has left the soil.

These first waterings are very important. The root ball directly beneath the trunk should never be allowed to dry out. Roots left dry will callus over and not take in water. On the other hand, too much water will rot the roots. Adding water on top of water is like wrapping the root ball in a wet blanket. Check every day, twice a day in warm weather, to determine when most of the moisture has left the newly added soil and air has reached the newly cut roots. As new growth begins to show, slowly (over a period of weeks) move the tree into the amount of sun the species requires.

Japanese bonsai masters have pointed out that when we walk outdoors we do not look up at the top of a tree, nor do we stare down at the base of the trunk. Instead, we walk along, looking ahead into the heart of the tree. At first it may seem difficult to work on your bonsai when it is elevated on an upturned pot, yet that is the best way, perhaps the only way, to design from the heart of the tree. As early as possible, try to develop the habit of working on a tree that is elevated on an upturned pot.

FIG. 27
This photograph shows what the tree could look like after a short period of continued pinching, pruning, and wiring. With work and time the tree will become more refined, with a thicker trunk and thicker branches. From the branches you will get many twigs and twiglets, developing planes of foliage.

6

Forests, Groves, and Saikei

Your bonsai experiments do not have to be limited to single plants. Multiple planting is a creative and fun way to utilize inexpensive materials. In this book, multiple plantings are referred to as forests and groves.

Forests and groves basically differ in the number of trees used. A forest utilizes many trees, so many that the actual number is not important. A grove usually has as few as three trees, or as many as eleven, but always an uneven number. This is because an uneven number of trees is easier to position in a natural way. An even number, on the other hand, often looks as if the trees were lined up by man, not created by nature. In a grove the eye is able to discern the approximate number of trees, which should all be of the same species.

When you are selecting material for a multiple planting, you can use smaller, less expensive trees. However, your dominant tree, the one on which the planting is centered, should be chosen with great care. This tree should have the thickest trunk and the best branch arrangement. The other trees need not be perfect, and probably would not be good enough to make a single bonsai.

Look for trees with different heights and trees with trunks of different thickness. If the trees' heights are too similar, adjust them by pruning. The variation in the thickness of the trunks enables you

to create perspective. Though trunks can vary in thickness, they should all be of the same line, that is, all straight or all slanted in the same direction. If some of the trunks need wiring to conform to the line, wire them before planting.

Before you plant your landscape, arrange and rearrange the trees until you are satisfied with the overall design. Create this design by giving the most prominent place to your dominant tree. For a more natural arrangement, avoid placing the dominant tree in the center of the container. Position the other trees so their trunks are visible. Do not place one tree directly behind another, and do not plant trees where their trunks might cross in front of another's.

The strongest branching should occur on outside trees and, of course, at the tops of trees. The design of a multiple planting is created by the line formed by the outside trees and treetops, as though the entire planting were a single tree. It is important to remember that the foliage on the top of trees in a forest shades the rest of the branches. You do not see as many branches on the trunks of old trees growing together. To create a similar effect in a multiple planting, you may want to cut back inner branches.

Containers used in forest plantings are necessarily large, to allow for the numerous trees and also to create unplanted land area. As these containers hold more soil than a regular bonsai container does, you should check different areas of the container to determine if the trees need to be watered.

When you finish your forest or grove, refer to the section Care of a Newly Potted Bonsai in Chapter 5.

SAIKEI

A *saikei* is a miniature landscape composed of rocks, trees, and often a riverbed of rocks or sand. For *saikei* you can use smaller, younger, and less perfect trees, material that would probably not develop into a first-rate bonsai. The landscape you create can represent a mountainous area, a coastal region, or even a desert scene with succulents. As with bonsai, with *saikei* you should strive to reproduce what is found in nature.

Containers used for *saikei* are often oval trays, brown and unglazed. The tray should be shallow, but large enough not just for the trees, rocks, and riverbed but also for open space. Miniature houses, animals, or figurines can be included, but they should be used with care.

Material used for regular bonsai is appropriate for *saikei*, but is usually smaller and younger. Trees should be of the same species, of assorted heights and trunk sizes. Material with a bare side can be planted with similar material, allowing the bare areas to mesh. As in other multiple plantings, the trunks in a *saikei* should all be in harmony, that is, all straight or all leaning in the same direction, as though the wind has bent them.

Rocks used in *saikei* should be compatible with the plants used, ones that could appear together in a natural landscape. Rocks should not look as though you simply placed them on top of the soil. To look both natural and old, they should be emerging from the earth. If only a portion of the rock is available, it invites the imagination to guess its size. Large rocks should be placed in the empty tray before the soil or trees. Florists' clay placed on the bottom of a rock and pressed against the bottom of the container should secure the rock.

Arrange and rearrange the rocks and trees until you create the landscape you envision. Wire the trunks of the trees if they need it. Branches too should be wired, pruned, and pinched as necessary. If any grasses or accent plants are used, be certain they have the same care requirements as the trees.

The care of a *saikei* planting is a little different from that of a bonsai. *Saikei* trays hold more soil and will not dry out as quickly as most bonsai containers. Water according to the trees' needs. If your trees need a little dryness between waterings, be sure to check several different parts of the landscape to be certain there are no wet areas of soil.

FIG. 28
The trees used in this saikei *are* Chamaecyparis pisifera squarrosa glauca, *a species of cypress. Growing from the rock are a clump of dwarf mondo grass and miniature creeping fig.*

Care of Bonsai:
A Five-point Program

An important consideration in selecting bonsai is that species vary in the amount of attention they require. Still, whichever species you choose means a commitment of your time. If you cannot envision checking and watering your plants regularly, then the joy of bonsai may not be for you. But taking care of bonsai is not all that difficult. By paying attention to five important points—light, soil, water, temperature, and humidity—you should be able to meet the environmental needs of most plants.

LIGHT

Light is the most important factor governing your trees' health. Photosynthesis proceeds at the appropriate rate if your tree is in the amount of light proper for that species of plant. Too little light will slow down the rate of photosynthesis. The lack of nutrients will damage the tree's health, affecting production of new growth as well as the nourishment of existing foliage. New growth will be weak and elongated, with greater space between the leaf nodes. The foliage will become larger, as the plant develops a larger leaf surface to trap more light. Trees in too little light use much less water than usual, another sign of poor lighting. Bonsai in too little light are easily overwatered, but not if you are checking the soil first and not simply pouring water into the soil by habit.

Indoor bonsai do not usually have the problem of too much light; however, if the sun is too strong, the leaves will burn, becoming scorched across the middle of their surface. These leaves will lose their rich green color and become pale green (a color not to be mistaken for the vigorous light green color of new growth). From too much light the foliage will press down, as though pushing away from light and heat.

Periods of Adjustment to Light Change

When trees recently root pruned are returned to normal light after a period of recuperation, they need a period of adjustment. Also needing adjustment time are newly purchased bonsai being introduced to a different environment.

Indoor bonsai that are moved outdoors should be acclimated to stronger light slowly. Once they are outdoors, gradually move them from shade into partial sun, and, if the species requires it, into full sun, until the desired amount of light is reached. Trees outdoors, receiving more light and moving air around them, dry out faster than plants indoors. Check for water daily, twice a day in hot weather. When preparing to bring trees back indoors, move them into less sun for two or three weeks to give them a period to acclimate to less light.

The move inside will be less stressful to your tree if you keep in mind you are changing its environment. For one thing, the light indoors is never as intense as that outdoors. With the changes in light, temperature, and humidity, the trees' water needs will also change. Do not water automatically; instead, check the soil to be sure the tree is ready for water. Also, to increase humidity begin misting on a daily basis.

Once you move a tree inside, decide the best location for the tree, then leave it there; do not move the tree from spot to spot or it will never adjust. Bonsai like *Serissa foetida* will have a few yellow leaves whenever you change its position, whatever light it is in. Just let it adjust to its new setting. Other species too may have a few yellow leaves for one or two weeks. This is normal, but you should always remove discolored foliage, so you will know if and when discoloration stops.

To allow the best light to reach all parts of the tree, turn your bonsai at least once a month. Turning is especially important when you grow plants indoors on a windowsill.

Artificial Light

In areas where outdoor bonsai are in storage from late fall to early spring, growing indoor bonsai has become more common. Artificial lighting can give your trees light during the winter, but taking plants indoors presents special problems. Heating outlets are sometimes located directly under windows, creating drafts of hot air that dry trees out. Incandescent bulbs also give off too much heat, which means you cannot place trees too close to that type of lighting.

Fluorescent tubes, the coolest lighting available, are your best indoor light source. They are readily available and are also the least expensive to operate. Plants utilize the same rays from fluorescent tubes that they do from the sun. In terms of the color spectrum, the blue rays keep plants healthy and compact,

Fig. 29
Ficus neriifolia, *willow leaf fig, will thrive in a sunny window. This tree tolerates a little dryness.*

and the red and the far red rays promote flowering.

There are several lengths of fluorescent tubes available, with the four-foot and eight-foot models being especially popular. All tubes lose a great deal of light output over time and need to be changed every year. Prices vary greatly. Some fluorescent "plant tubes" are expensive and do little more for plants than cool white (fluorescent) or a combination of cool white and warm white. If space is available, use two four-foot tube fixtures and a reflector. The light intensity drops off greatly two to three inches from each end of the tube, no matter what kind of tube you use. With artificial light, there are no dark, gray days; instead, everyday is the fourth of July and it's always noon. Artificial light allows you to do the following:

1. Provide strong, consistent light.
2. Control the length of the day, and thus the flowering of trees by providing longer days.

3. Set up trays under the lights, thus making watering easier. This is especially true if there is a bed of stones in the bottom of the tray for excess water to drain into. The bottom of the bonsai container must be kept dry. Set the tree on an upturned pot to keep it above the water. This arrangement creates a more humid area, a great benefit to trees.

4. Group trees, thus making them easier to care for.

Place trees so their tops are six to eight inches from the fluorescent tube. If the new growth is overly large or leggy, consider placing the trees closer to the tube or lengthening the hours of light. Ten to twelve hours is a good starting point that should keep your trees healthy and compact. If flowering does not occur, increase light time by several hours. As consistency of the light is important, consider purchasing a timer to turn lights on and off.

Bonsai growing under artificial light go into dormancy, but in most cases the dormancy is unnoticeable. Remember that for trees growing under lights, every day is a sunny day. Such trees often require more water than trees on a windowsill. Watch for new growth, a sign of an active tree. If plants are actively growing, they may need fertilizer.

SOIL

A problem that many beginners have is trying to use too many different soil types. Remember that growing four bonsai in four different or unknown types of soil calls for four times the amount of thought and care.

It is easier to grow bonsai when you use a soil mix you are familiar with. Knowing which soil mixture your plant is potted in helps take some of the mystery (and some of the danger) out of bonsai. Review the Soil Mixes section in Chapter 4, which explains what the compo-nents of a soil mixture do. Keep a record of when a bonsai was last potted and the amount of new soil added so you can anticipate root development. If you acquire a new species that requires dryness between waterings, remember that you can add coarse sand for faster draining and dryness. With soil mixes there is no mystery, as you simply make the adjustment to the mix, an option you do not have with prepackaged potting soil, which usually does not list ingredients.

WATER

Japanese bonsai masters believe it takes years to learn to water bonsai properly. Unfortunately your trees cannot wait years for you to learn this skill. And no one else will be able to give you a useful watering schedule. If you are given one, view it not as information but as misinformation. Still, watering is an art that can and must be learned because most plants are lost to overwatering, and many others dry out, usually because their pots are too shallow. Teach yourself proper watering by learning all you can about the needs of your bonsai, and by seeking out information from other bonsai people, horticultural societies, and your garden center. Experienced gardeners can tell you how to water a camellia, even if they have no experience with bonsai camellias. Adjust such general information about watering to the confines of your bonsai container, which will dry out faster than a garden-center container.

Always water a plant from the top, as this allows water to come out through the holes in the bottom of the container. The plant will receive the water it needs, and salts and chemicals that have built up in the soil will be washed out of the pot. With a tree that is planted high, with the soil mounding upward from the edge of the pot, the water often runs off, missing the container. Go over the tree three or four times with the watering can until some water has come out of the bottom of the pot.

Variations in Watering

The origin of the plant is a clue to its water needs. Obviously plants from a rain forest have different water needs than plants from a desert. Also, plants' water needs change with the temperature. The warmer the air, the more water a plant needs. When air is cool, plants require less water. In cool, damp weather, do not overwater, especially during dark, rainy spells. Plants also have different water needs at different growth stages.

Dormant plants should be watered less, but even dormant plants need enough water to keep the root ball from drying out. During active growth plants use more food and water and need to be watched more closely. Plants setting flower buds need more water, less when the flowers open. Finally, plants change with age; older trees grow more slowly.

Junipers and pines require dryness between watering wherever they are—in the ground, in a nursery, or in a bonsai container. The important difference is that a juniper in a container does not have extra soil to act as a buffer if the tree does not receive water on time. You must water it at the first sign of dryness.

Moss used as ground cover is another factor affecting watering. When moss covers the soil, the soil is not exposed to the air and does not dry out as quickly. Moss often feels dry when the soil is not. Pick up a corner of the moss to feel the soil before watering. Water if the soil is dry, but not if only the moss is dry.

A newly potted bonsai, one with new soil around the root ball, will dry out more slowly than when it was rootbound. With bonsai in need of repotting, the roots fill the pot. There is no extra soil around the roots, and the tree requires more and more water. When you notice a plant needing more water, you should root prune and repot the plant.

Overwatering, which causes roots to rot, can be a long, slow process. The decline of the tree is gradual and often not visible for a long time. One sign of too much watering is large weak growth. (Large weak growth is also caused by too little light.)

Another sign of overwatering is dry foliage that appears over a long period. Because the foliage feels dry, you may think it is due to lack of water. However, the key is that the dryness has occurred over an extended period, usually because of the slow rotting of roots.

Trees are harmed less by a little dryness than from too much water, but be careful that your plants do not dry up. At times total drying out occurs, and the tree is lost. Other times the drying out is partial, only the foliage is lost, and you may be able to save the tree. Foliage approaching the danger stage of being

Fig. 30

Buxus microphylla compacta Kingsville, *Kingsville boxwood, requires some sun. Water as it starts to feel dry, that is, when a great deal of water has left the soil but some moisture remains. The inner root ball directly under the tree should not dry out.*

too dry appears dull and has lost its shine. This is most obvious with serissas and azaleas. Bonsai in this condition should be misted, watered a little, then given a complete watering several hours later.

If foliage is limp, check the condition of the soil. If the soil is wet, the problem is overwatering. If the soil is dry, water and mist the plant the same way you would dull foliage.

TEMPERATURE

Some trees grow in all temperatures but others are much less tolerant. Your selection should be made according to your ability to provide temperatures needed by those species. This is especially important when you grow indoor bonsai during the winter. A sunny window is usually fine for subtropical and tropical material.

HUMIDITY

Humidity is an important factor in growing tropical bonsai indoors in the winter. In the northeast and other cold areas of the U.S., houses are extremely dry during winter months. There are various ways to adjust the humidity to improve your plants' chances of survival:

1. Use a humidifier.
2. Mist foliage daily with tepid water. Mist lightly, and be careful that you do not allow drops of water to form on the foliage and drop into the soil.
3. Group trees together.
4. Grow trees on a tray or saucer with a layer of stones lining the tray. Keep bottoms of the bonsai containers dry, and do not let them sit in excess water. However, keep water in the tray, as it will evaporate around the tree and increase humidity.

In outdoor areas that have heavy dew at night, do not wet the foliage during the evening hours. In dry areas of the country, where some species of plants may prove difficult, rely on local advice.

PESTS

The same pests that harm other plants also harm bonsai. Avoiding pests is the best policy, since it is easier to prevent problems than to save plants infested with insects. If you develop an insect problem, segregate the tree. Wash the infested tree, then wrap the pot to the trunk level in aluminum foil or plastic, and spray the foliage with any kind of liquid soap and water. Seek further advice at your garden center.

Avoid the pest problem by shopping in places that are clean, bug-free, and where all material looks healthy. When making a selection, look the plant over carefully. Especially check the backs of leaves for insects or signs of insect damage. Chewed foliage is a sign of bugs.

Upon arriving home with a new plant, go to the hose or sink and wash the foliage. Afterwards, each time you water the plant, also wash the foliage. Clean trees will not allow a pest problem to take hold. But be careful of overwatering. Wash the tree only when you water it.

Bonsai, with less foliage and more open growth, are easier to keep clean than regular plants. Another advantage of bonsai is that you can hold a bonsai in your hand and look at it from all sides. Remember that observation is an important part of keeping trees healthy.

There are many products on the market to deal with insects, and your garden center can make helpful recommendations. However, if trees are kept clean by frequent washings, you may never have the pest problem. To keep your collection clean and healthy, do not introduce new acquisitions directly into the area of your trees. Keep them segregated for several weeks, as you observe and wash them.

Root Pruning and Repotting

Bonsai is not a matter of squeezing all the roots of a plant into a container and then shaping the top growth. The relationship between the roots, the top growth, and the container must be in balance. Root pruning and repotting are techniques essential to maintaining this balance.

ROOT PRUNING

Many trees are lost because root pruning is done at the wrong time of the year. Although root pruning can be done anytime except when the plant is dormant, spring is the best time for root pruning your trees. Until you become comfortable with the root-pruning process and familiar with the material you are working with, it is safer to root prune in the spring. As a rule, indoor bonsai grow faster than outdoor bonsai and may require root pruning more frequently. Generally, it is safe to remove one-third of the roots. Concentrate on removing the heavier new roots. Remember that it is the hairy, fibrous roots that nourish the tree and keep the root system young and vigorous.

REPOTTING A BONSAI

Repotting an established bonsai is never as difficult as creating a new bonsai. The reason is fairly simple: the roots of a rootbound tree are the exact shape of the container, while the roots of a plant in a nursery pot bear little resemblance to the shape of the bonsai pot. Of course, you have to know when to repot a plant. The following are indications that your bonsai is ready for repotting:

1. Roots are growing through the screen that covers the drainage holes in the bottom of the bonsai container.

2. The tree dries out more quickly than it should.

3. The tree is growing fast, is full of healthy growth, and requires frequent pinching. These are signs of a fast-developing root system.

4. The roots seem to have raised the tree in the container.

FIG. 31

The roots in the sketch have consumed all the potting soil, leaving no loose soil to fall off.

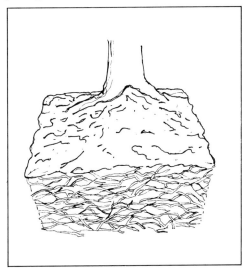

F<small>IG.</small> 32

Exposed roots radiating from the trunk add a sense of strength and age to a bonsai. A bonsai with strong, exposed roots looks like it has survived hurricanes, blizzards, and whatever else the elements presented. These desirable roots are not usually present in young material but develop with age.

If you observe any of those signs, look at the plant's root system. Do not hesitate to look at a tree's roots. Too often beginning students fear that looking at the roots will harm the tree but that is not true.

To look at the roots, do not pull the tree out of the pot. The best and easiest way to find out if a tree is rootbound is to turn the container over and gently slip the pot off, a procedure that does not harm the tree. It is much better to check the roots often, in this manner, than to allow the tree to go into decline. Young bonsai should be checked every year. As trees age, the interval between repottings becomes longer.

If no roots are visible and you see only soil, return the plant to the pot. But if the roots have spread to the edge of the soil or across the bottom of the soil, and no loose soil falls off, it is time to repot.

The best time of the year to repot is spring, when trees are most active and send out new roots and top growth quickly. If a tree is rootbound in the fall, repotting can be risky. Rather than repot, it is better just to add a pad of fresh soil under the root system. Of course, repotting the plant should be the first thing you do in the spring.

To repot, place the bonsai on the work bench, and remove the moss and loose soil from the top of the root system. Use a rake or tweezers to rake across the top, down the sides, and across the bottom, removing old soil. Look at the root system and remove the heavier new roots.

Trimming the roots allows you to repot the tree in its original container. Before doing that, wash the pot to remove any remaining roots and debris. You can slip a tree in and out of a clean pot without damage to the root system. If a pot is not clean, the roots will grow into the old soil and the tree will not slip in and out easily and safely. After washing the pot, replace the screen, then add stones and a pad of soil according to the potting procedure described in the section At Home in Chapter 5.

While you have the plant outside the container, keep the exposed roots moist by misting them. When you place the tree back into the container, spread out the roots on all sides. Be sure to repot with a fresh soil mixture, and chopstick the soil into and around the root ball as needed.

If there are wires on the tree, make sure they are not too tight. Do not allow wire to grow into the trunk or branches. Be sure to use wire cutters to cut wire. Do not try to unwind wire, as that can damage the bark. You also run the risk of breaking the branches you've been carefully training.

Pinch new growth, not only to refine the tree but also to conserve the tree's energy. Follow the instructions given in the section Newly Potted Bonsai in Chapter 5.

Seasonal Changes

Many bonsai need water every day, sometimes twice a day, so you should check them often. And summer heat and wind cause bonsai to dry out more quickly than usual. As days grow longer, bonsai also grow more hours a day. They use up and need more water. Also, with longer days and more active growth, plants should be fertilized. Watering also washes needed nutrients from the soil, so you may want to review the section Fertilizer in Chapter 4.

As days become shorter, growth slows down and bonsai use less water. At this time, plants are preparing for the dormancy of winter. The rest of this chapter and the explanation of winter storage of outdoor trees in the Bonsai Containers section of Chapter 4 should help you meet your plants' winter needs.

OUTDOOR TREES IN WINTER

In many areas of the world bonsai require no special winter storage. Bonsai in warm areas remain outdoors during the winter, just as they do during the rest of the year. However, these bonsai do experience some degree of dormancy.

In cold areas that experience only occasional frost, trees should be grouped together and mulched with leaves, peat moss, or marsh hay. Mulch prevents evaporation of water from the soil and freezing of roots. Spread the mulch under and around the containers, and also place one or two inches on top of the soil. Do not cover the foliage, as air circulation is important.

In areas with harsh winters, you must place your plants in some sort of winter storage, as in one of the following:

1. In an unheated basement or attic that remains cold and where the temperature does not fluctuate a great deal.

2. In an unheated greenhouse. Again, be certain that the temperature does not fluctuate. Greenhouses are usually built in the sun, so be sure to watch the temperature.

3. In the garage. Place the trees on a bed of mulch in a shallow tray with drainage holes. Fill in the area around the containers with mulch and also place one or two inches of mulch on top of the soil.

4. In a cold frame, that is, an unheated, boxlike, plastic- or glass-covered structure for protecting young plants. These structures are easily constructed, and various plans are available.

5. In the ground. Where it is possible, this is an excellent way to store trees in winter.

Prepare the spot before frost by digging a hole the shape of your container, and about two inches deeper and two inches wider than the container. After a hard, killing freeze, place the tree on a two-inch bed of mulch, then place mulch around the container and over the top of the soil. Do not cover the foliage. Select

an area where the foliage is free from drying winds and where snow does not slide off a roof, in other words, an area where the tree will remain cold and dormant. A sunny spot can cause a thaw and freezing, neither of which is desirable. The purpose of storage and mulching is to keep the temperature constant.

An important advantage of outdoor storage is that trees do not have to be reintroduced to the elements. By being outdoors, dormant trees go into and come out of dormancy naturally, adjusting smoothly to changes of temperature and length of day. In contrast, trees coming out of garages, cold frames, etc., should be watched carefully. A sudden exposure to wind can cause the tips of branches to dry and die back.

All trees should go into winter storage with soil that is moist but not soaking wet. Water plants a day or two before placing them in storage. Throughout the winter, check the stored trees, and if they are dry, water them. Watering should be done in the morning so excess water will drain out during the day, before night falls. A long, unseasonable winter warm spell requires more frequent checking of stored trees' water needs. They should return to total dormancy when the cold returns.

INDOOR TREES IN WINTER

In areas where tropical material will not survive winter temperatures, trees must be brought indoors. Bring your trees inside before the windows in the house are closed and the heat is turned on. This will allow them to adjust to the house climate more easily. The trees may or may not become dormant, but they will keep their foliage and require good light. In most cases a sunny window will suffice. If artificial light is used, refer to the section Artificial Light in Chapter 7.

Indoor bonsai are not always dormant during winter, and dormancy is not always easy to identify. If a bonsai continues to send out new growth, it is not dormant but merely growing at a slower rate than at other times of the year. An indoor dormant plant is often described as "looking fine, but doing nothing." A plant holding its foliage and color but showing no new growth is in a state of dormancy, manufacturing food and using only enough water to maintain its health. At this time be careful that you do not overwater your bonsai. As a general rule, remember that throughout the year the amount of light received and the amount of water needed are in direct relation to each other.

Trees going into outdoor winter storage and, more important, trees being moved indoors should be clean and free of insects. Areas to check are the foliage, both top and bottom, under the rim of the pot, and the drainage holes. If you find a problem, ask your local garden center for advice. Remember to wash the foliage when you water the tree.

Advanced Techniques

Once a tree is growing as a bonsai and the container has become its home, changes will occur. The first root pruning, if done correctly and accompanied by the removal of top growth, is a great stimulus for the tree to develop a pot full of feeding roots. With many species, especially fast-growing indoor trees, this can happen at the end of the first year.

When a young tree is in a container, the restricted room and feeding (for health, not growth) cause thickening of the trunk and slowing down of the branches' growth. In time the leaves become smaller but the flowers and fruit do not reduce in size. At this stage, as a bonsai begins to show refinement and develop character, much of the time you previously spent on root pruning, repotting, and constant pruning and pinching can be spent on fine pinching and general refining.

When you began working on your bonsai, it may not have had roots under the soil radiating from the trunk, the kind that eventually become "exposed roots." As such roots may develop with time, check to see if candidates for "exposed roots" are present when you repot a tree. However, do not expose them unless you are certain they will make the tree appear older and stronger.

THICKENING TECHNIQUES

Under certain conditions trunks and

branches will thicken more quickly than usual. This is important to know because thick trunks and good branch structure form the very heart of bonsai artistry.

Stock material planted in the ground will thicken more quickly than material kept in pots. In the ground a plant will likely develop a taproot, primarily to keep it upright, as well as feeding roots. To some extent, you can control the root development of your plants.

Dig a hole two inches deeper than the size of your plant, then place small stones in this two-inch area. Place a piece of screen over the stones, then plant your tree. Make sure the soil level remains constant; do not plant the tree deeper in the hole than it was in the container. The stones and screen will keep the new roots shallow and will inhibit growth of a long taproot. Every other year, measure an inch beyond the spread of the foliage and use a spade or trowel to cut straight down into the soil to prune the roots in the ground. This action results in a compact root system and a thicker stock to work on.

While the plant is in the ground, some pruning and shaping can begin. However, keep in mind that thickening the trunk and branches is the main purpose of planting the material. A trunk that is allowed to grow taller will develop a thicker base to support the taller growth. Later on, you can prune the top of the trunk to create an older-looking and thicker-trunked tree. A trunk also thickens in proportion to the number of branches it has to support. In other words, the more branches to support, the thicker the trunk becomes. The same principle applies to the thickening of branches. The more foliage a branch has to support, the more the branch thickens.

Plant material that cannot be grown in the ground because of adverse weather conditions can still be thickened by being placed in larger pots with ample soil. Your only concern here should be not to overwater the plants. An additional advantage of using larger pots is that you will be relieved of a great deal of the daily watering that plants in smaller pots require.

JIN AND *SHARI*

Accidents do happen and sometimes a branch is broken or dies, often for no apparent reason. Do not be too quick to cut off the dead or damaged branch, as it can add the appearance of age to your tree if you make it a *jin*, a dead branch or dead portion of a branch from which all the bark has been stripped. When you create a *jin*, try to preserve all the twigs, as they can add to the design of your plant. To create a *jin*, you will need *jin* pliers, described in the section called Introduction to Tools in Chapter 4. Practice creating *jin* by splintering and peeling the bark from branches cut from trees outdoors.

A dead portion of trunk that looks as though it has been struck by lightning is called *shari*. To create a *shari*, use the *jin* pliers to separate the bark from the trunk. When you make either a *jin* or *shari*, do not prune the branch or the trunk. Use the pliers to squeeze or crush the bark of the branch or trunk you are working on. Peel back the crushed bark to the core of the branch. Then grasp the tip of the peeled branch and pull at it to create a rough tear that looks as if it happened naturally.

For the present, view the creation of *jin* and *shari* as ways of dealing with accidents to your bonsai. Intentional creation of *jin* or *shari* should come only when you have considerable experience with trees.

DEFOLIATING

Defoliating is a technique used to speed up the production of smaller leaves on deciduous bonsai. With time, all deciduous trees will produce smaller leaves but defoliating accomplishes the process sooner. However, it must be stressed that only very healthy trees should be defoliated, and a newly root-pruned bonsai should never be defoliated.

Defoliating is best done as soon as the tree has leafed out. Remove the leaf and its stem except for the very base of the stem, which must be left on the tree to avoid injuring the bud that is located there. The tiny piece of the stem that is left dries up and falls off by itself.

In parts of the country with a short growing season, defoliation should be done as soon as the tree has leafed out, but to no more than one-third of the tree in any one season. In southern climates, with much longer growing seasons, it is easier to defoliate because trees in warmer areas have a longer time to produce new leaves.

A totally defoliated tree should be kept in bright shade and out of the wind until the new buds swell. At that time the tree can be moved into the sun, and new leaves will come in small. Partially defoliated trees can remain in the sun.

Defoliating is not a technique to try casually. Unfortunately, it is something that many novices want to try. We urge you to wait and be certain that you really want to try defoliation, and then only on very healthy trees.

Varieties
of Bonsai Trees

The following lists include only a small portion of the hundreds of plants used for bonsai. Most plants described here are readily available in most areas.

OUTDOOR BONSAI

Acer   maple

There are numerous varieties of maples used for bonsai. Leaves range in size from small to large, and in shape from almost round to the deeply cut, thread-like varieties of the Japanese maple. Through the spring and summer the foliage can vary from the lightest yellow-green to the deepest burgundy. Some varieties have highly variegated foliage, with three or four colors on each leaf. In autumn, maples turn color, and the landscape is painted gold, orange, and red. Their magnificent colors make up for maples' short growing season and the extra effort required for outdoor bonsai.

Maples can withstand a half day of sun, but noonday sun and a drying wind are hard on them (and on most trees, in general). Maples' thin leaves and shallow bonsai pots can result in leaf burn during hot spells. Check maples frequently and water them as needed. As was recommended in Chapter 4, extra peat moss can be added to the soil mix. Pinching and pruning help develop compact growth and shorter spaces between leaf nodes.

Fig. 34

Trees that bear fruit make attractive bonsai. These include species of orange, quince, cherry, and this crab apple.

Where maples grow naturally, seedlings come up everywhere, often where you don't want them, like in your front lawn. Dig them up and pot or plant them in an area where they can be watched and tended as future bonsai. Patches of seedlings can be removed in clumps and replanted as groves or forests.

Acer buergerianum   trident maple

One of the most popular and certainly the most photographed of the bonsai maples, the trident maple has beautiful bark, shiny green foliage, and brilliant autumn colors of orange and red. The leaves reduce in size considerably after

FIG. 35

This Catlin elm is a fine example of a bonsai in the curved upright style.

defoliation or as the tree grows as a bonsai. With age, the trident maple develops magnificent roots radiating out from the trunk.

Acer palmatum   Japanese maple

Highly prized for landscapes as well as bonsai containers, the tree called Japanese maple includes many varieties, from full-leaf to the feathery-leaf version that looks like lace. *Acer palmatum* is a hardy plant but the most highly cut, rarer varieties should be avoided by novices.

Carpinus   hornbeam

Several varieties of hornbeams can be developed into bonsai. Young material that lacks strong branching makes nice group plantings. Hornbeams, like maples, are sensitive to drying out.

Chaenomeles   flowering quince

Flowering quinces are tolerant of a wide range of conditions and respond well to root pruning and top pruning. They can be used for single trunk bonsai, but because they grow naturally in clumps, you must constantly cut new growth coming from the ground. This same trait makes flowering quinces ideal for multiple plantings. They flower in many colors, some varieties producing different colors on the same tree.

Chamaecyparis   false cypress

The foliage of false cypress varies from deepest green to lightest blue-green, making this an interesting tree. False cypress responds quickly to pruning and pinching, and tolerates root pruning with minimum stress.

Chamaecyparis obtusa   hinoki cypress

Hinoki cypress requires a great deal of pinching, pruning, and wiring in its development stages. Some varieties of *Chamaecyparis obtusa nana* grow slowly, have small foliage, and make outstanding bonsai.

Chamaecyparis pisifera glauca blue moss cypress

This tree is a good bonsai subject that benefits from an attractive blue-green color.

Cotoneaster   cotoneaster

These small, woody shrubs, with their strong, angular growth, require heavy pruning in the early stages. Many lend themselves best to semicascade and windswept styles. Tiny white flowers and bright red fruit appear on the tree at the same time. Cotoneasters like to be dry between waterings.

Juniperus   juniper

Junipers can be trained in all styles and sizes of bonsai and thus are appropriate for people of all levels of ability. Junipers are excellent material for the novice because they respond with vigor to all techniques, budding up easily on hardwood. For experienced people, junipers are excellent subjects for advanced techniques like the making of *jin* and *shari* (discussed in Chapter 10).

Junipers require sun, and should be

dry between waterings. A few varieties, especially *Juniperus procumbens nana*, can be kept indoors during the winter. With indoor junipers, pay close attention to water needs, and if you're in doubt, wait until the next morning to water. Place junipers in a sunny window, and keep in mind they like daytime temperatures in the sixties. Junipers can also be put into outdoor storage.

Rhododendron azalea rhododendron

A number of miniature rhododendron make fine bonsai. One that is especially hardy in colder regions is *Rhododendron moerheim*, which becomes woody and has small leaves and lavender flowers.

Azaleas (of both indoor and outdoor varieties) are nice to work with because they become woody, and many develop fine trunks and good branch structures. They take root pruning, respond well to pinching and pruning, break new buds on old wood, and are comfortable in small pots. Another advantage is that azaleas give wide choices of size, color, and shape of flowers. Disadvantages are that branches tend to be brittle, and the bark is easily scarred during wiring.

Satsuki azaleas, many with variegated and striped flowers, are very popular. Choose varieties with small leaves and flowers. Although it takes many seasons of pruning and shaping to develop a treelike structure, satsuki azaleas are well worth the time.

After blooming, azaleas (like most flowering plants) go into their strongest growing period. This is the time to root prune your plants if they need it. Prune and reshape the top growth that may have become shaggy during flowering. Wire any plants that need it. Wire them carefully, remembering that a tree is more flexible if it is slightly dry.

Azaleas and rhododendrons do best in several hours of morning sun; noonday sun should be avoided. Water as they start to feel dry. Check your plants often when they are actively growing, as they use a lot of water. If you pruned the azalea right after it flowered, you can pinch the new growth lightly. But do not pinch the next spurt of new growth, as that growth will set new flower buds for the following season.

Indoor azaleas can be put out in late spring and then left out in the fall. Outdoor azaleas should go into winter storage.

Because azaleas and rhododendrons vary in their cultural needs, learn which ones are best suited to your area.

INDOOR BONSAI

Subtropical and tropical trees that will not survive outdoor cold become indoor bonsai during the winter. Indoor bonsai should be placed next to a sunny window; their watering needs are covered in the sections on watering in Chapter 7 and the section Indoor Trees in Winter in Chapter 9.

Bougainvillaea bougainvillea

Bougainvilleas are most attractive in cascade or semicascade styles, where flowers are shown off to their best advantage. Prune the branches back severely after the plant flowers. In very warm weather keep the container in a saucer of water; however, in winter when bougainvillea is indoors, let it get a little dry between waterings.

Buxus boxwood

Woody boxwood makes fine material for bonsai. Choose trees with very small leaves and compact growth.

Buxus microphylla compacta Kingsville boxwood

Kingsville boxwood is the aristocrat of indoor bonsai. It has a rich, dark color, small foliage, and develops heavy wood

Fɪɢ. 36

Azaleas are one of the most popular bonsai trees. Even without its pretty flowers this tree makes an attractive bonsai.

when relatively young. It can be developed into all styles of trees but is most often seen as either a straight or slanting upright. It takes root pruning and top pruning, and responds well to wiring. In every way Kingsville boxwood is a fine choice.

When a boxwood starts to feel dry, water it thoroughly. This tree is sensitive to careless watering that reaches only part of the roots, so watering must be thorough. Boxwoods are tolerant of a little more or little less light, but never full sun.

Calliandra   powder puff

Powder puff is an attractive plant with pink flowers. It likes the sun, should not be allowed to dry out, and should be pruned after flowering. Branch development is slow. The dwarf variety is best because it has small leaves and flowers.

Camellia   camellia

Camellia shrubs and trees can be easily wired into several upright styles to show off their beautiful flowers. Many people prefer varieties with smaller leaves.

Camellias do best in only morning sun. They should be watered just as they start to feel dry and should not be allowed to dry out. Camellias thrive in a humid atmosphere.

Carissa   carissa

Also called the natal plum, carissa has white flowers, red fruit, and dark green leaves. It is a good subject that naturally tends to spread but with pruning becomes compact. Carissa needs a lot of sun to produce flowers, so a sunny location is the place to grow it. Water as it starts to feel dry.

Cuphea hyesopifolia   elfinherb

This small shrub has small leaves and charming pink flowers. It requires severe pinching after flowering and should be placed in a sunny window. Do not allow it to dry out.

Ficus   fig

Figs are ideal candidates for indoor bonsai. They are tolerant of imperfect light, of air that is a little dry or humid, and of most indoor temperature ranges (from the high fifties to the low seventies). Figs shed a little when the seasons change, but new growth appears immediately. Leaves reduce, but many varieties begin with smaller leaves, and many send down aerial roots.

Place your fig in the morning sun, and water it as it starts to feel dry. As it is fast growing, you will have to pinch and prune it as needed. When pruning, do not be alarmed if the tree weeps a white sap.

Ficus benjamina   weeping fig

Probably the most well-known fig, *Ficus benjamina* has large leaves (that will reduce) and develops thick surface roots.

Ficus diversifolia   mistletoe fig

The charm of this fig is the tiny fruit that remains on the tree for a long time. The color of the fruit changes from light orange to red. Small black dots on the backside of the leaves are part of the leaf and not insects.

Gardenia radicans   gardenia

Gardenias are loved for their beautiful and very fragrant flowers. Their shiny green foliage is also very pleasing. Gardenias should be pruned after they flower. They like warmth and sunny windows, and should not get too dry.

Malpighia glabra   Barbados cherry

Several varieties of malpighias make attractive bonsai, especially the small, curved examples. Pruning and pinching throughout the growing season produce more compact plants. Flowers and fruit are very nice. A sunny window and a little dryness between waterings keep malpighias happy.

Olea   olive

Though not easily found, the European olive makes an attractive bonsai. New growth must be pinched often, as branch structure develops slowly. This plant likes morning sun and should be watered when it feels dry.

Podocarpus   podocarpus

Podocarpus, especially the short-needle variety, is not easily found, but when available it makes fine bonsai material. It is very easy to live with, and will adjust to lower light if necessary. Water podocarpus when it starts to feel dry.

Rosemarinus   rosemary

Pruned often, rosemary develops into a nice tree. Grow it in a sunny window, and water it only when it is dry. Do not disturb the roots more than necessary, and then only in late spring.

Serissa   serissa

Serissa is an altogether pleasing plant, especially indoors. As a bonsai, it can be grown straight upright or slanting. Between periods of flowering it sends out a lot of new growth, which needs to be pinched. Young serissas are very flexible and can be easily wired.

Place serissa in a sunny window, and water it as it starts to feel dry. Yellow leaves may appear when the plant needs feeding or its location changed. Do not be alarmed and do not start overwatering. If the yellow leaves are from moving, let them adjust. If the plant has not been fed for three or four weeks, give it a high phosphorous feeding (15-30-15).

There are many varieties of serissa, including ones like the green-leafed serissa snow rose that flowers almost continuously. Many have variegated foliage that can be white- or yellow-edged. Serissa Mount Fuji has beautiful white variegation that calls to mind Japan's famous snowcapped mountain.

Ulmus   elm

Many elms make fine outdoor bonsai, but they require winter protection. However, the Catlin elm is an indoor tree, which, if placed in a sunny window and watered only when it's dry, makes a very pleasing bonsai. Bonsai elms are most satisfying when they are designed as elms in nature.

During winter's short days, many of which are cloudy, bonsai rarely get enough sun. Fluorescent lights solve many light problems during the winter. Outdoors for the summer most plants should get a half a day of sun. Morning sun is preferable, as there is no heat buildup; noonday sun should be avoided. As was mentioned previously, the instruction "water as it starts to feel dry" means you should water when a great deal of water has left the soil but some moisture remains. Of course, the inner root ball, directly under the trunk of the tree, should not dry out.

Common Questions about Bonsai

What is the best way to get started in bonsai?

Locate a bonsai club, attend a lecture or classes, read whatever you can. Most important, experiment. You'll learn more from hands-on experience than from anything else.

Do bonsai grow in the ground?

No. Bonsai are miniature trees grown in shallow containers.

Do bonsai have to be old?

No. It is the illusion of age that is desired. Accomplishing this with a young tree is great artistry.

Am I too old to start bonsai?

Certainly not. No matter how old you are, if you're interested in bonsai, you should not miss the joy of "finding a tree" in an overgrown stock plant, or the pleasure of selecting a bonsai you would like to have.

Are bonsai kept small by wire?

No. Wire is used only to help design a tree.

Do bonsai have to be wired?

Not necessarily. Wire is used only where it is needed. Many trees are never wired. Such trees are designed by pruning and pinching only.

Are bonsai kept small by lack of food?

No. Bonsai are fed to maintain health.

Are bonsai delicate?

No. Bonsai are strong, hardy trees.

Are bonsai difficult to take care of?

Not if you receive good instructions, especially about light and water needs.

Are bonsai easily lost?

Not easily, but they die when owners do not know how to take care of them or are not committed to their survival. To lose a tree and not know why is an unqualified loss. To lose a tree and learn why is an essential part of your education.

How often should I water my bonsai?

Watering is a complicated matter, depending on such factors as light, temperature, etc. You will have to learn watering on your own, but we have included some guidelines in this book.

How will I know if I'm doing something wrong to a bonsai?

If there is a change in the tree's appearance, seek help at once. The problem may be due to watering, poor light, or an environmental factor. The sooner the problem is corrected, the better the chance your tree will have to recover.